CHRISTMAS SOLOS FOR THE TRUMPET.

AMSCO PUBLICATIONS
NEW YORK/LONDON/SYDNEY/COLOGNE

Exclusive Distributors:

Music Sales Corporation
24 East 22nd Street, New York, NY 10010 USA
Music Sales Limited
8/9 Frith Street, London W1V 5TZ England
Music Sales Pty. Limited
27 Clarendon Street, Artarmon, Sydney, NSW 2064, Australia

International Standard Book Number: 0.8256.1162.8

Printed in the United States of America by
Vicks Lithograph and Printing Corporation

ANGELS FROM THE REALMS OF GLORY

Traditional

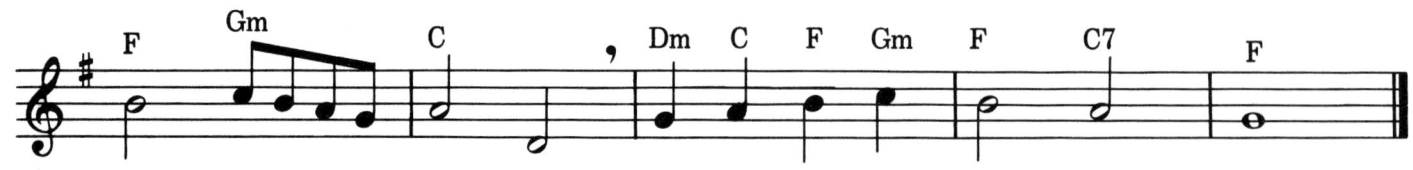

Abiding In The Fields
Traditional

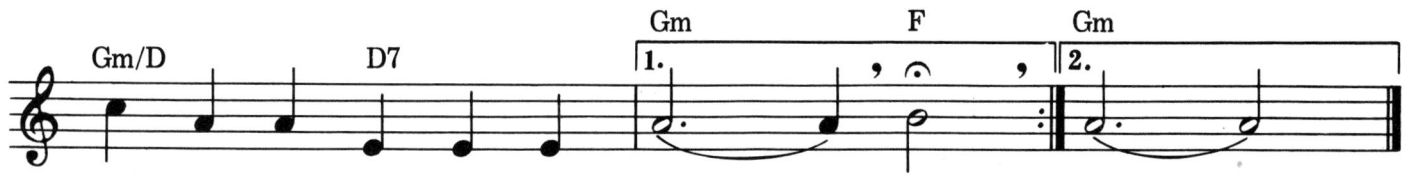

Away In A Manger (Version 1)
James R. Murray, 1841–1905

Away In A Manger (Version 2)
William J. Kirkpatrick, 1838–1921

A Child This Day Is Born
Traditional English carol

All My Heart This Night Rejoices
Johann G. Ebeling, 1637–1676

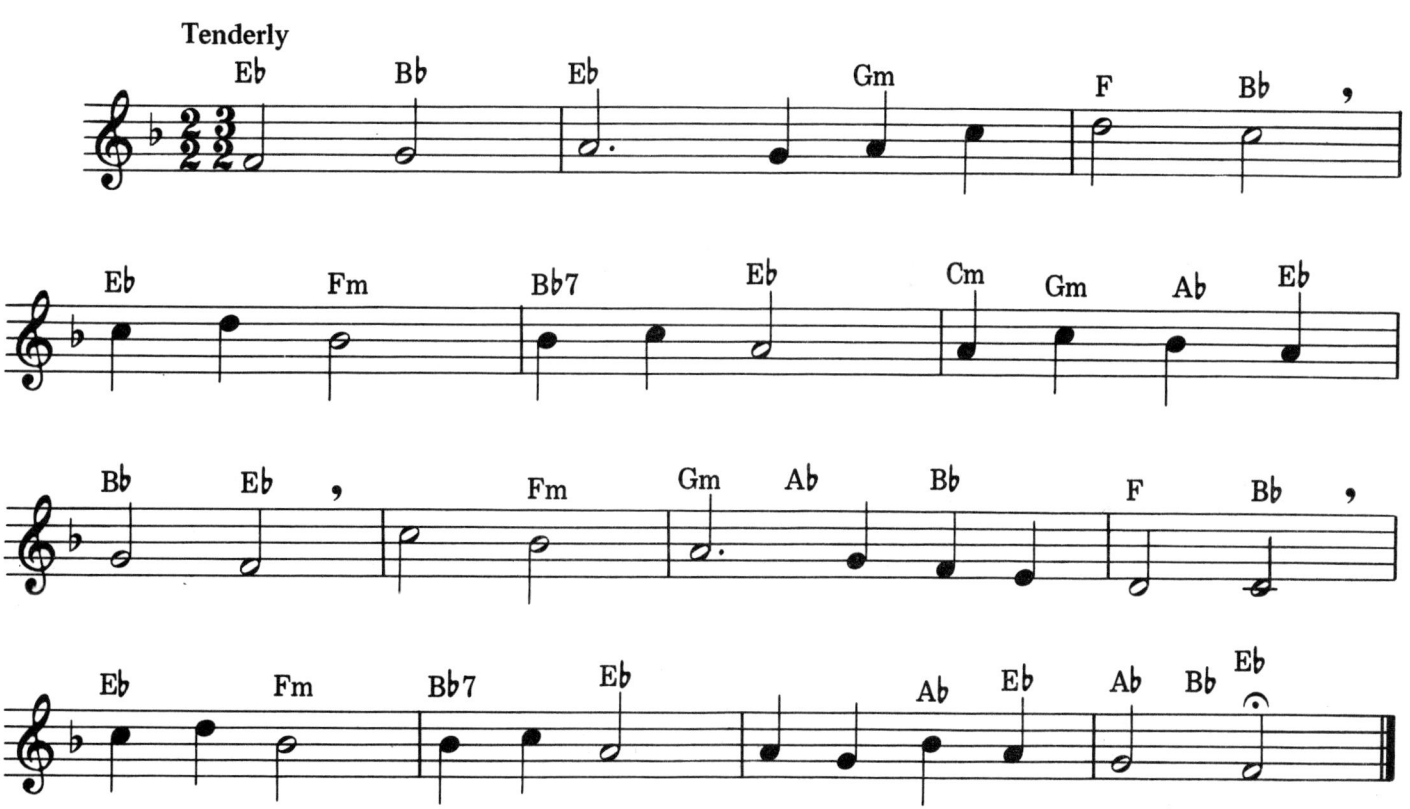

As With Gladness Men of Old
Conrad Kocher

The Angels And The Shepherds
Traditional

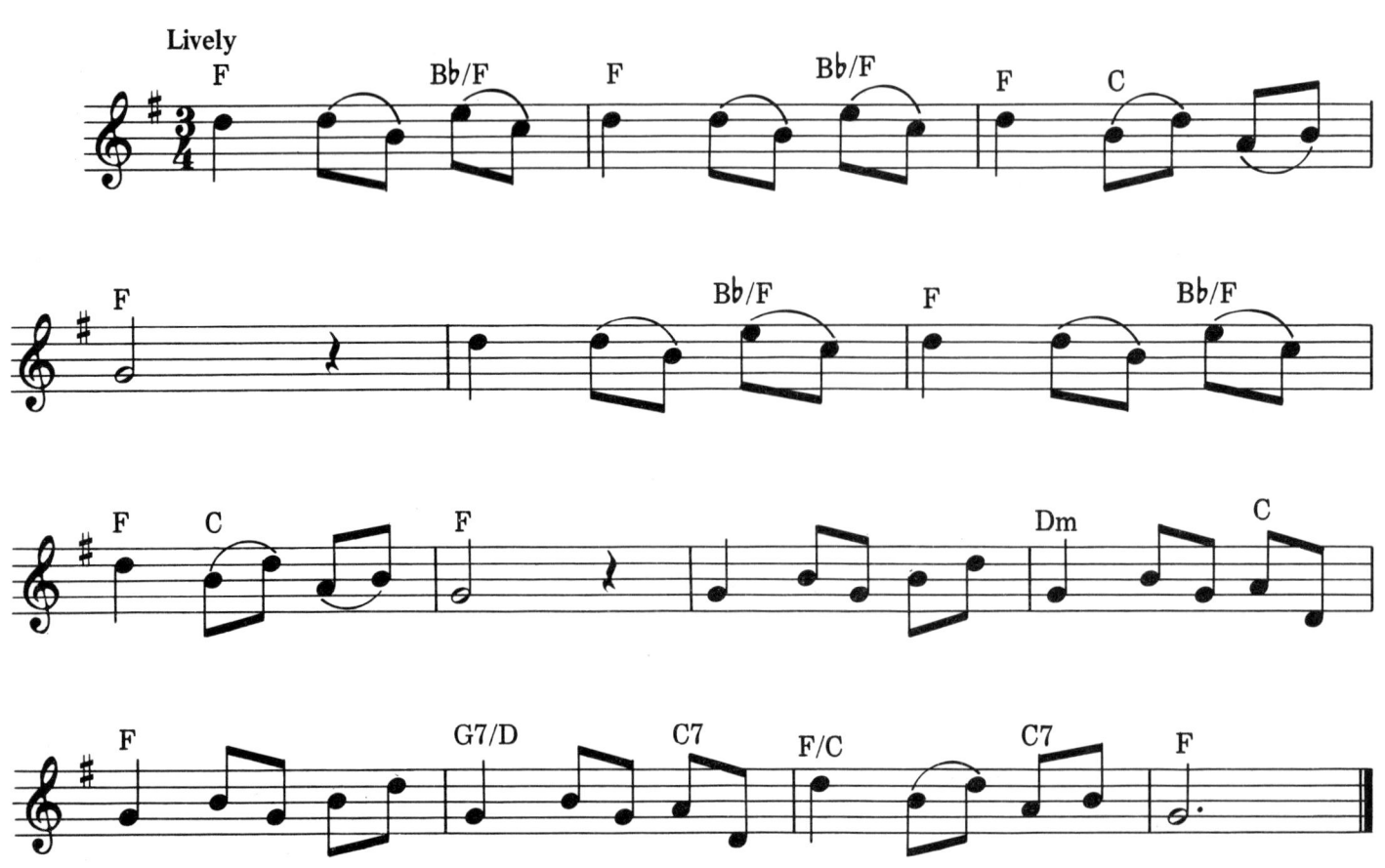

As Lately We Watched
Traditional

Angels We Have Heard On High
Traditional French carol

The Coventry Carol
Traditional

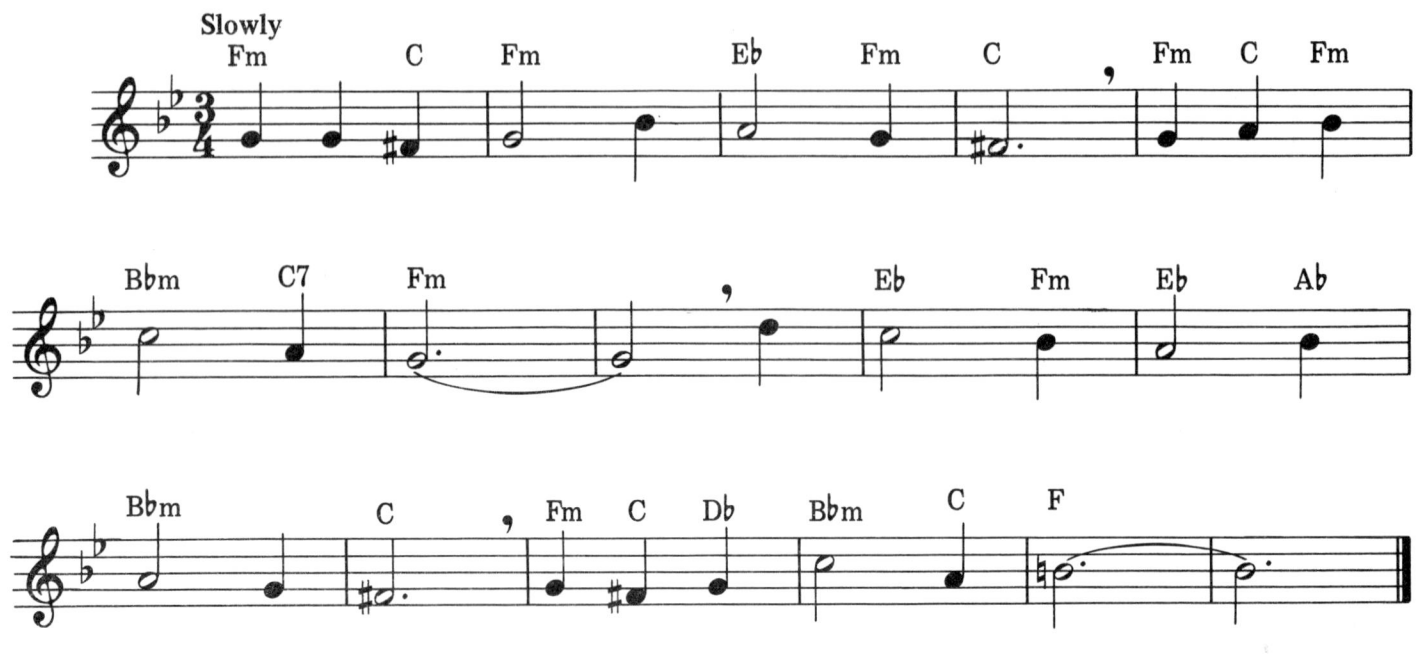

The Babe Of Bethle'm
from Rimbault's *Old English Carols*, 1865

The Angel Gabriel

Traditional

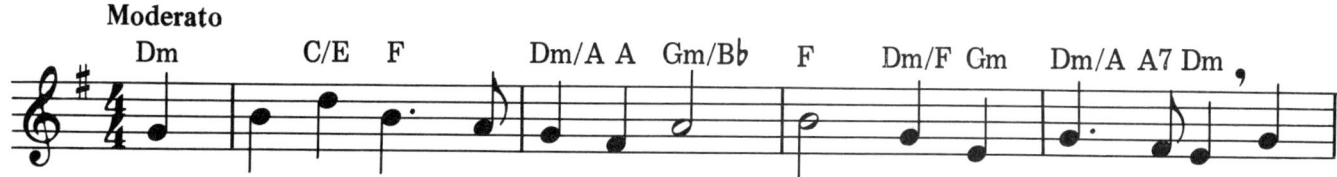

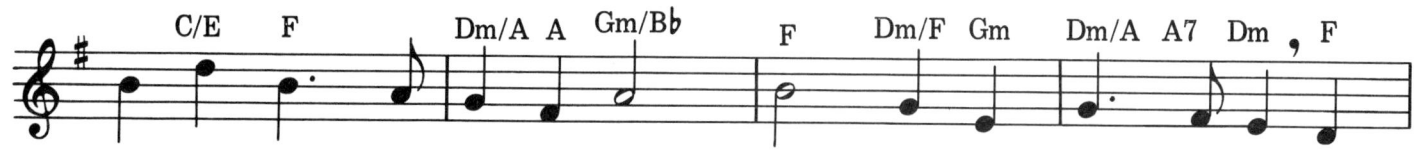

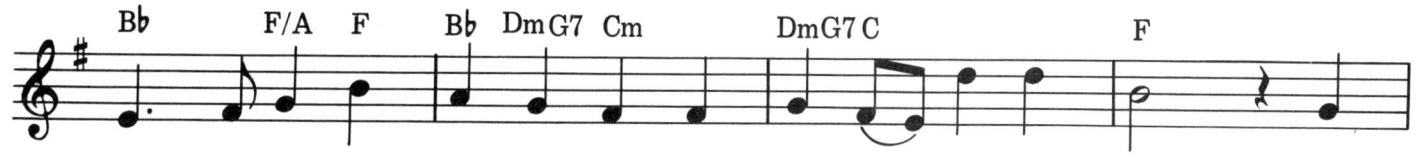

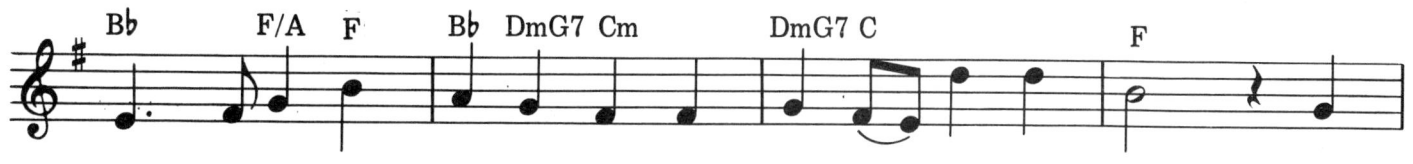

THE CHERRY TREE CAROL
Traditional

Moderato
No Chord

BESIDE THY CRADLE HERE I STAND
from Klug's *Gesangbuch*, 1535

Tenderly

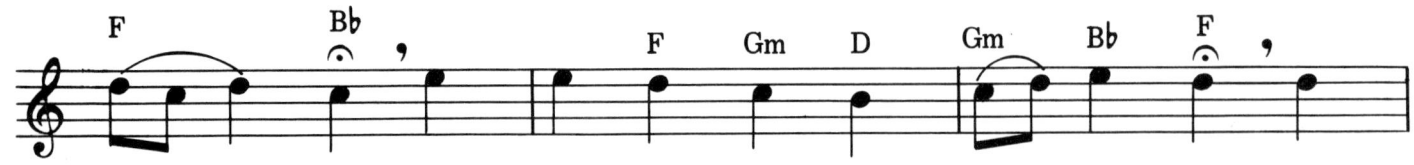

Ring Out, Ye Wild And Merry Bells
C. Maitland

Break Forth, O Beauteous Heavenly Light
Johann Schop, c. 1590–1664

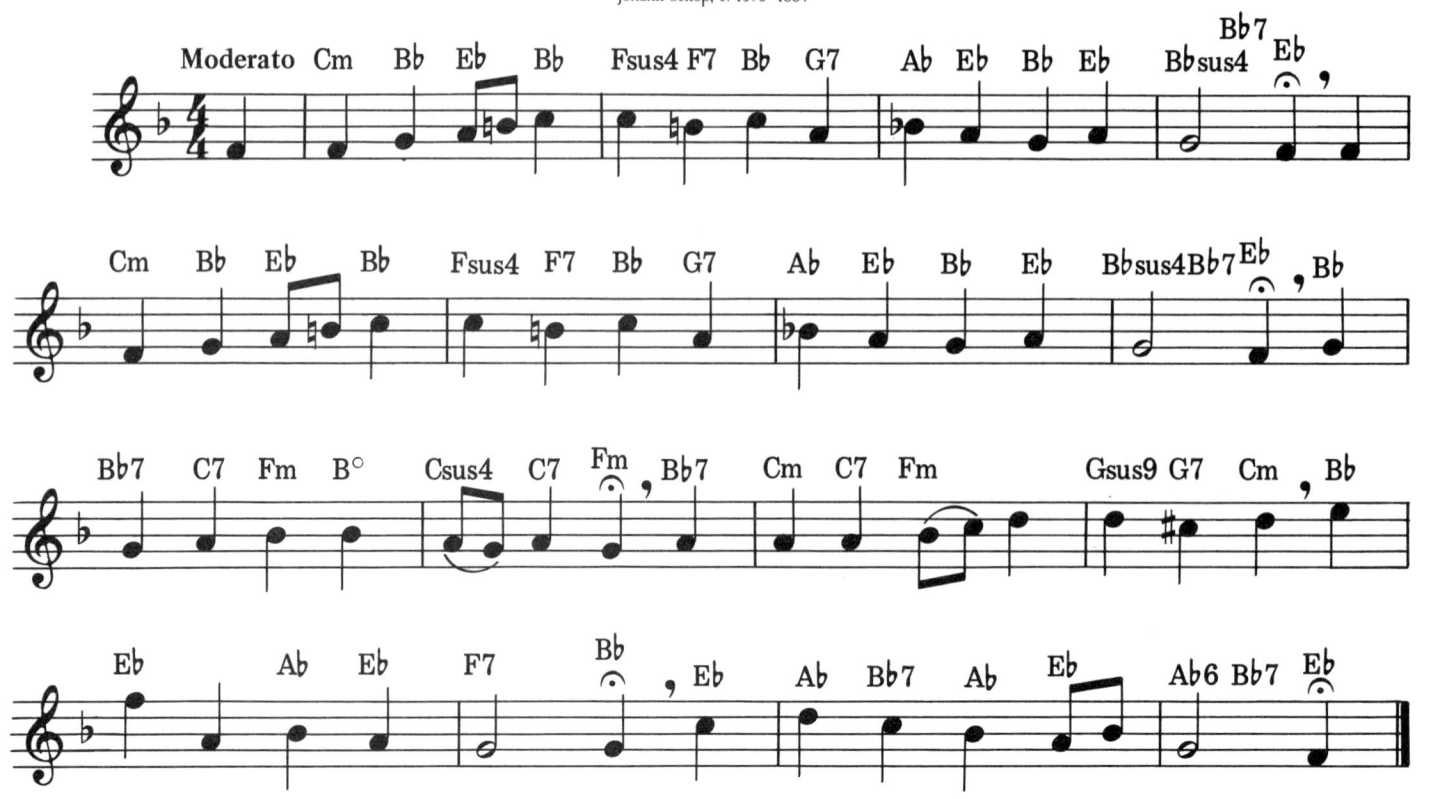

Brightest And Best
Traditional American carol

Bring A Torch Jeanette, Isabella
Traditional French carol

Christ Was Born On Christmas Day
Traditional American carol

Good King Wenceslas
from Theodoricus Petrus of Nyland's *Piae Cantiones*, 1592

The Cradle
Traditional

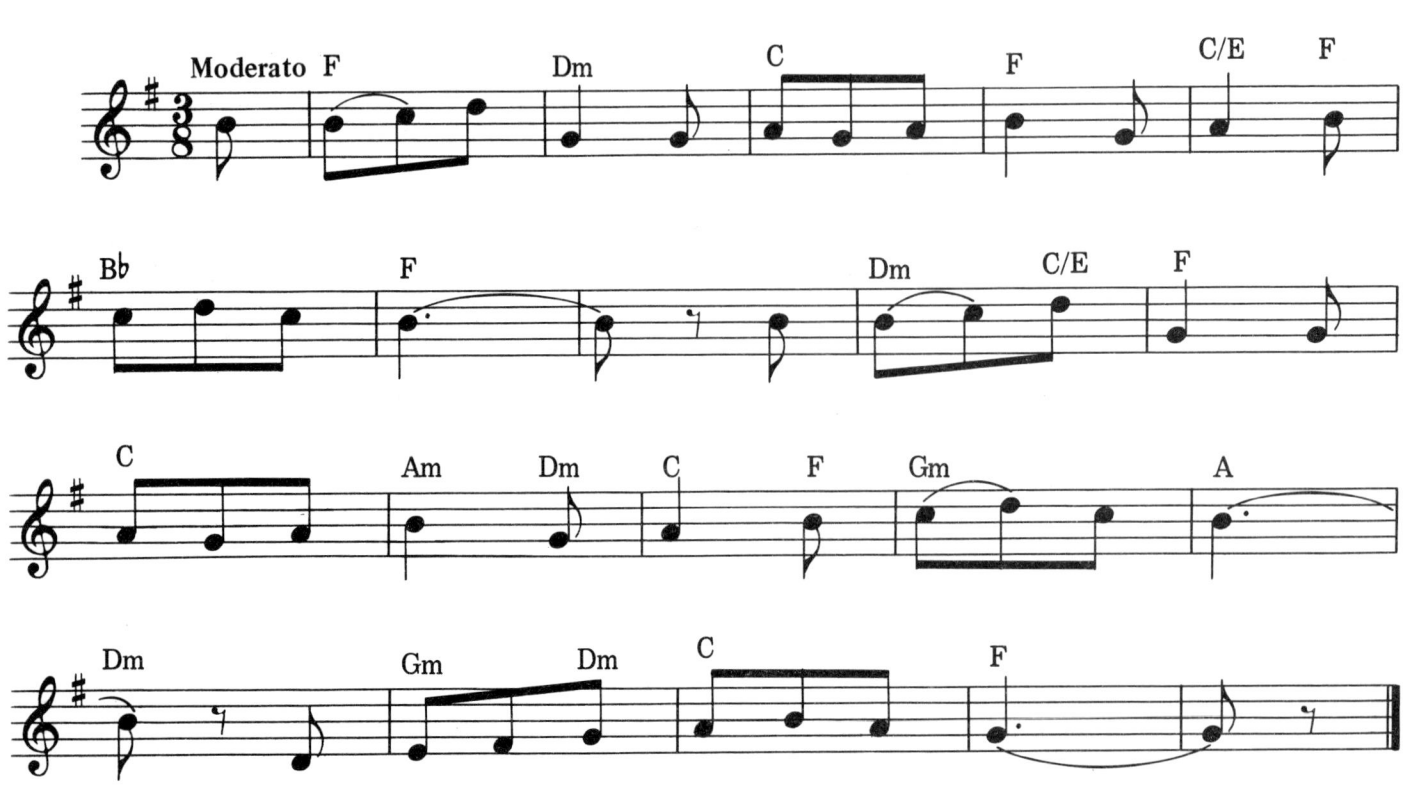

Christmas Eve
Traditional

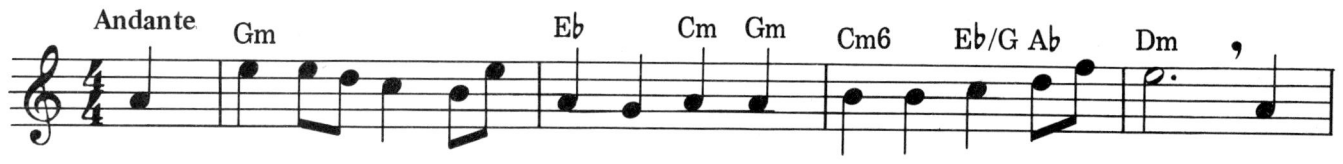

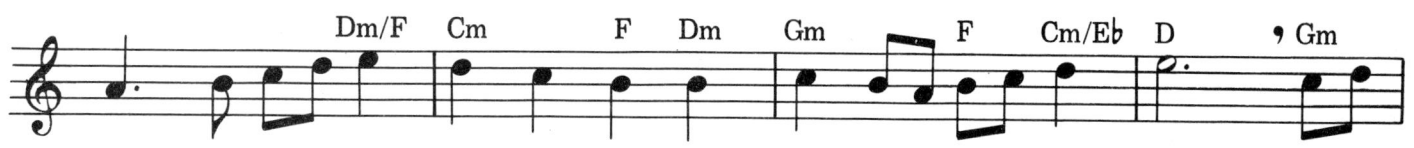

The First Nowell
Traditional English carol

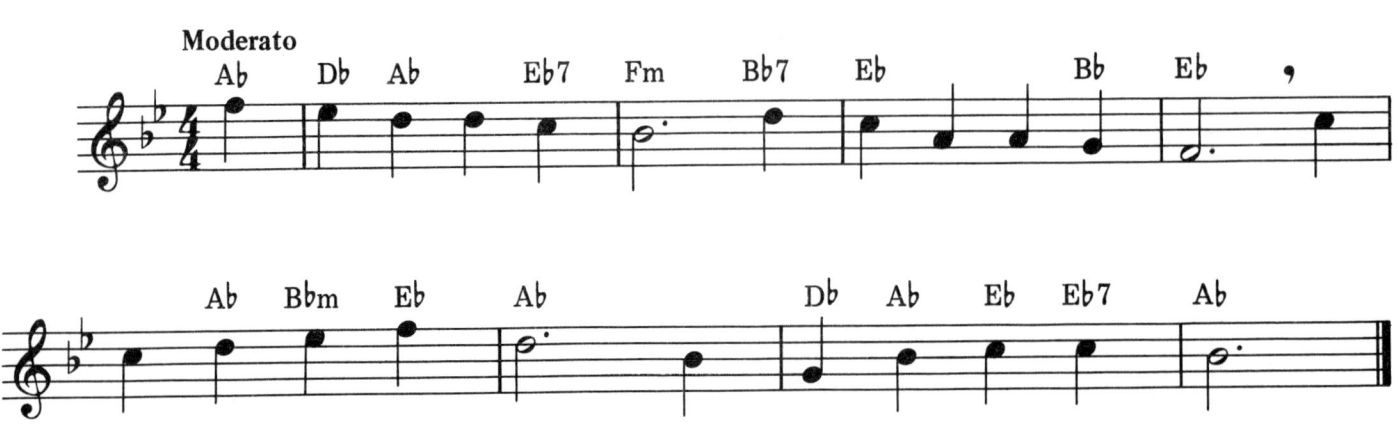

God From On High Hath Heard
Leighton George Hayne, 1836–1883

DECK THE HALL
Traditional Welsh carol

FLEMISH CAROL
Traditional

20

The Friendly Beasts
Traditional English carol

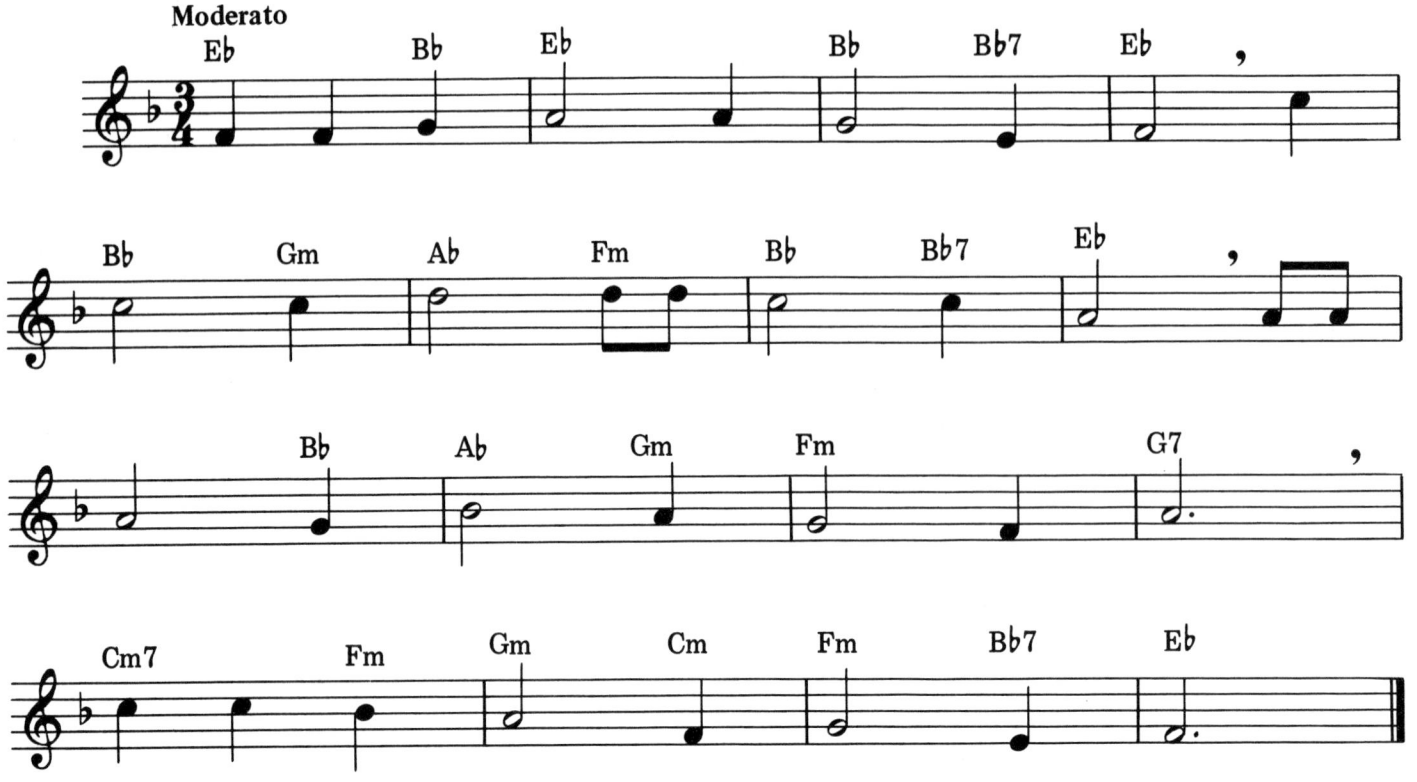

God Bless The Master Of This House
Traditional English carol

In Dulci Jubilo

14th century German tune

How Brightly Beams
Traditional

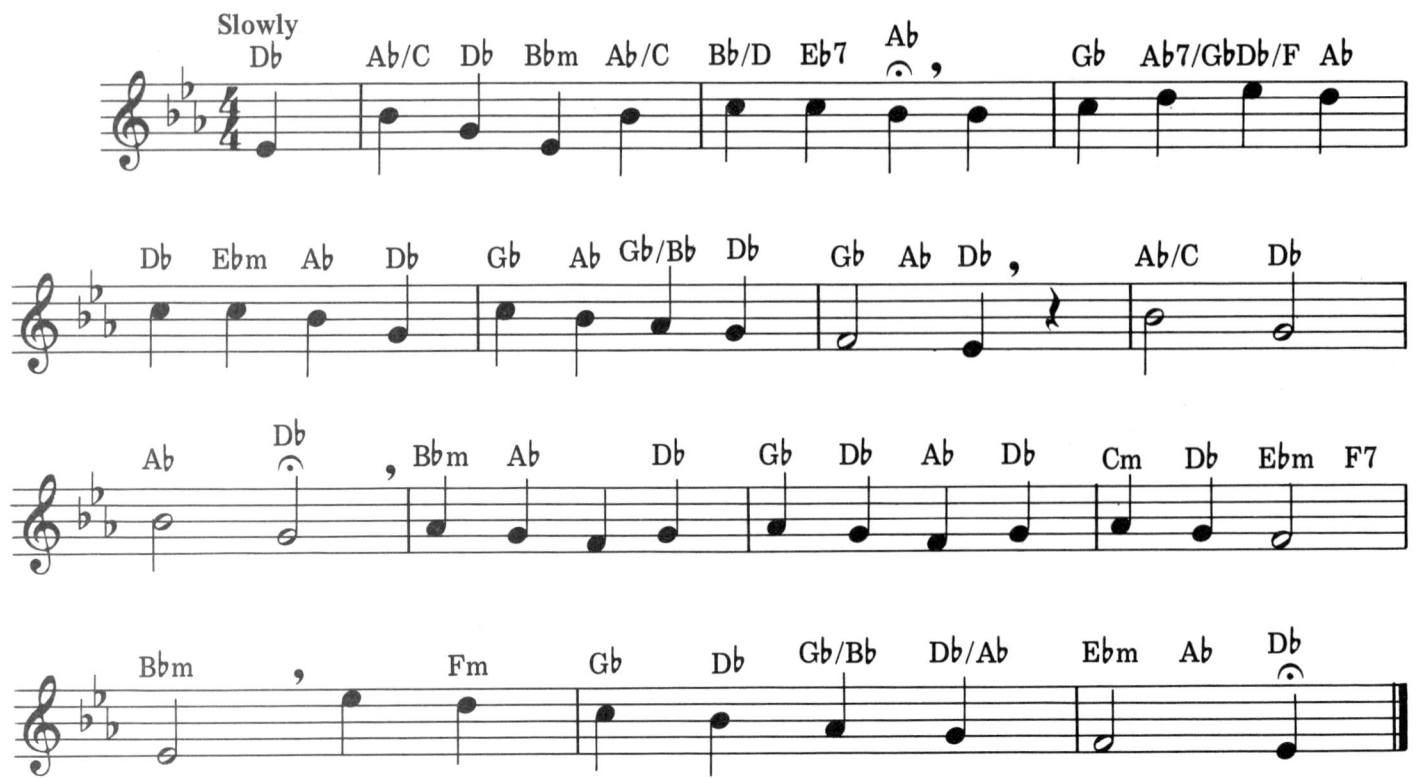

If Ye Would Hear
Traditional

There Came A Little Child To Earth
R.N. Mathews

Hark! The Herald Angels Sing
Felix Mendelssohn Bartholdy, 1809–1847

24

Here We Come A-Wassailing
Traditional English carol

Infant Holy
Traditional

The Holly And The Ivy
Traditional English carol

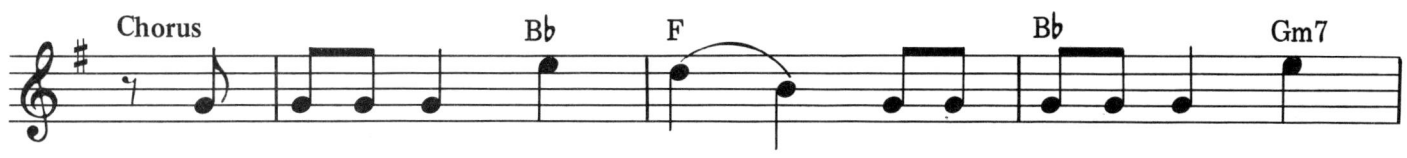

God Rest You Merry, Gentlemen
Traditional English carol

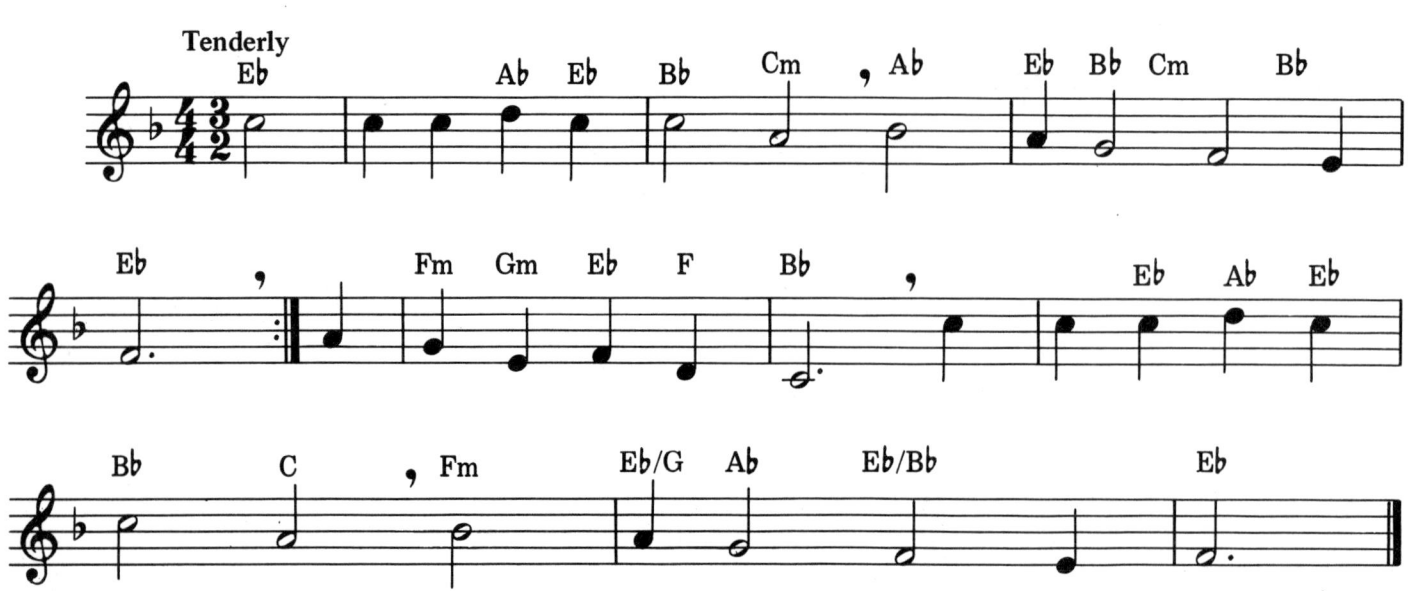

Lo, How A Rose E'er Blooming
15th century German tune

O Come All Ye Faithful
John F. Wade, 1711–1786

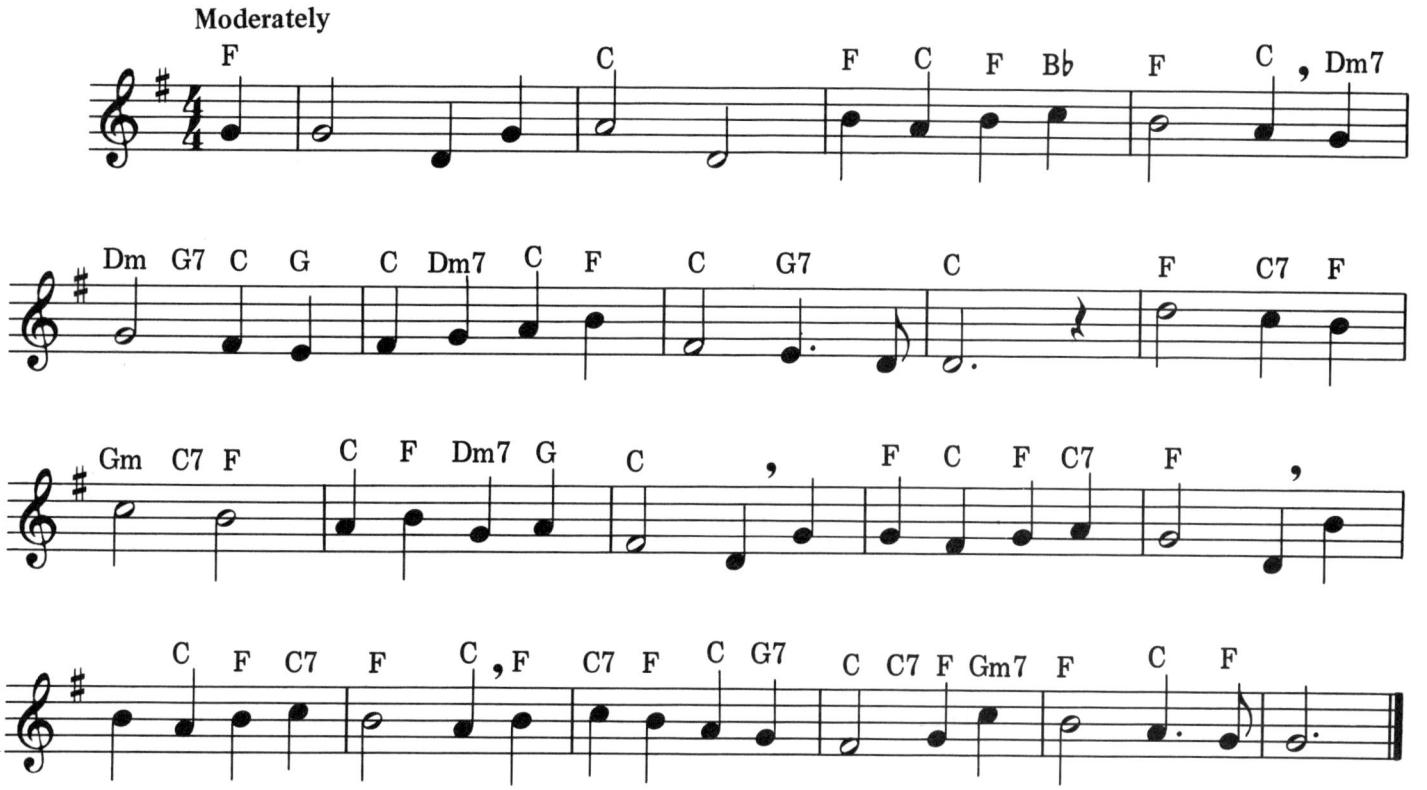

Once In Royal David's City
H.J. Gauntlett, 1805–1876

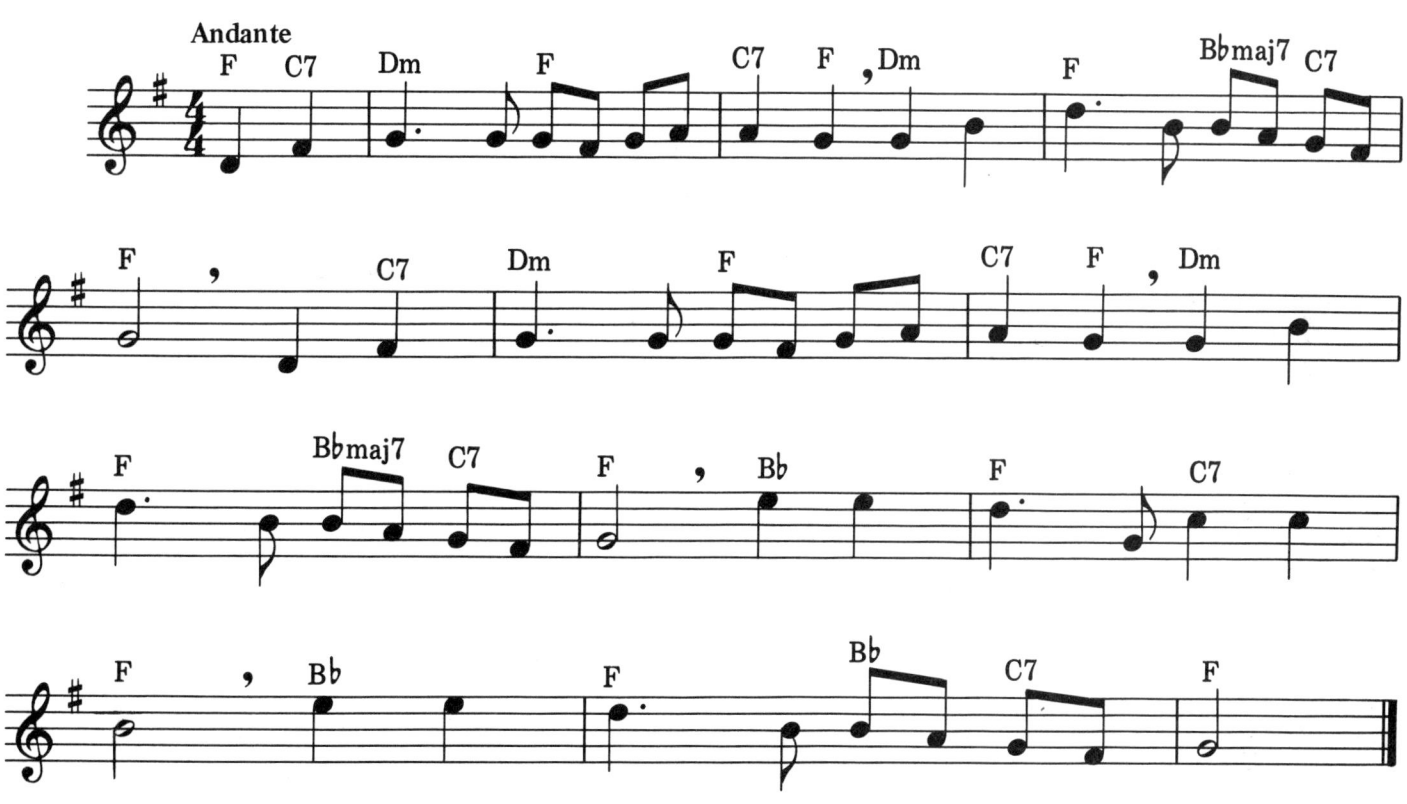

Joy To The World
attributed to George Frideric Handel, 1685–1759

Lully, Lully, Lo
Traditional

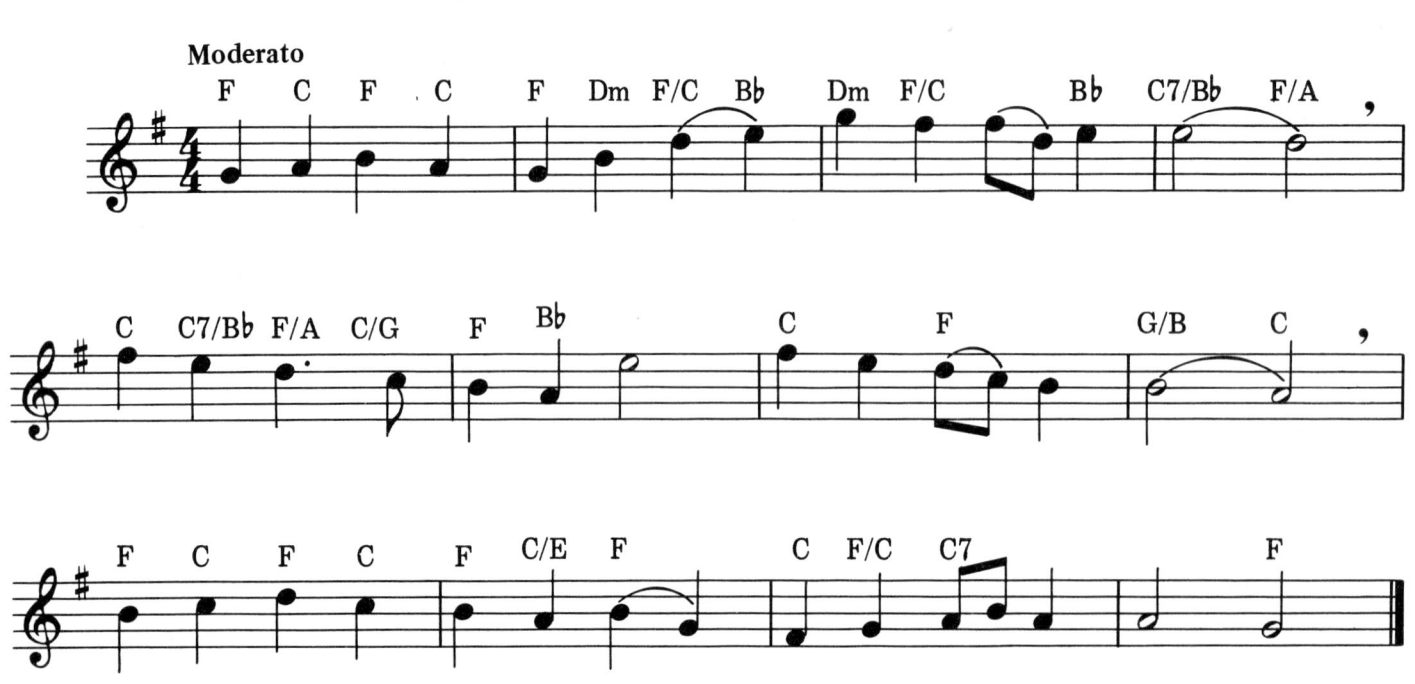

It Came Upon The Midnight Clear (Version 1)

Richar Storrs Willis, 1819–1900

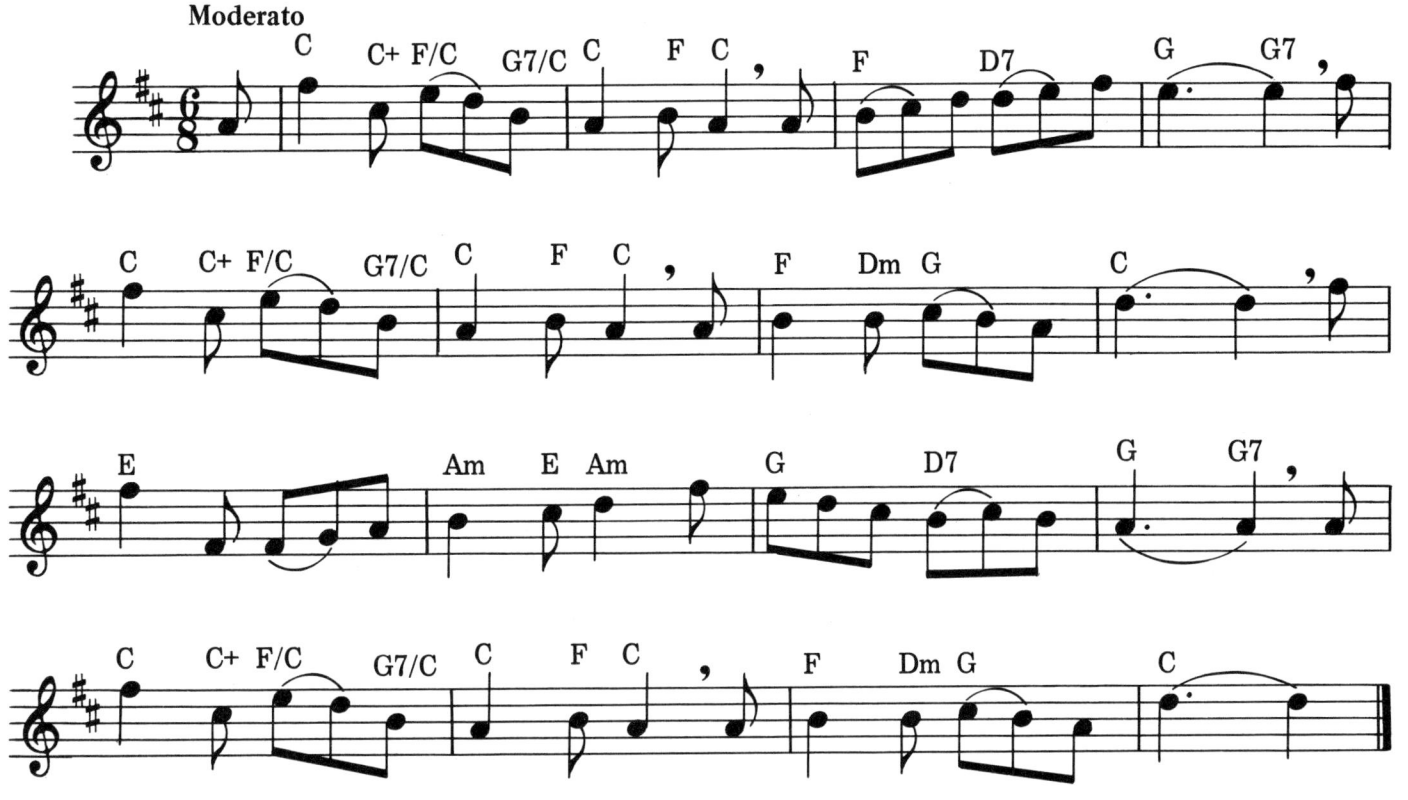

It Came Upon The Midnight Clear (Version 2)

Arthur Sullivan, 1842–1900

Let Our Gladness Know No End
Traditional Czech carol

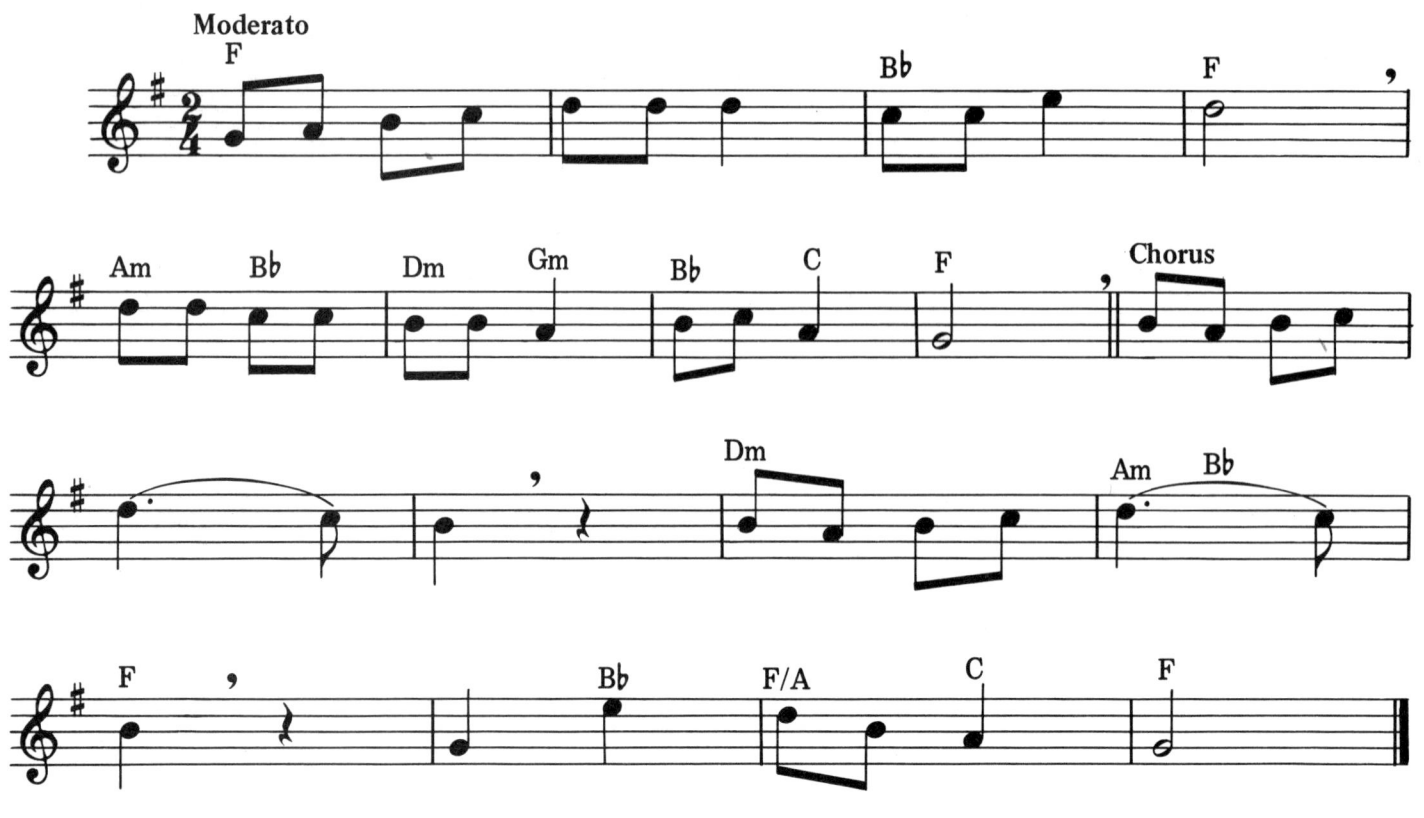

Mary, Dear Mother Of Jesus Divine
Traditional

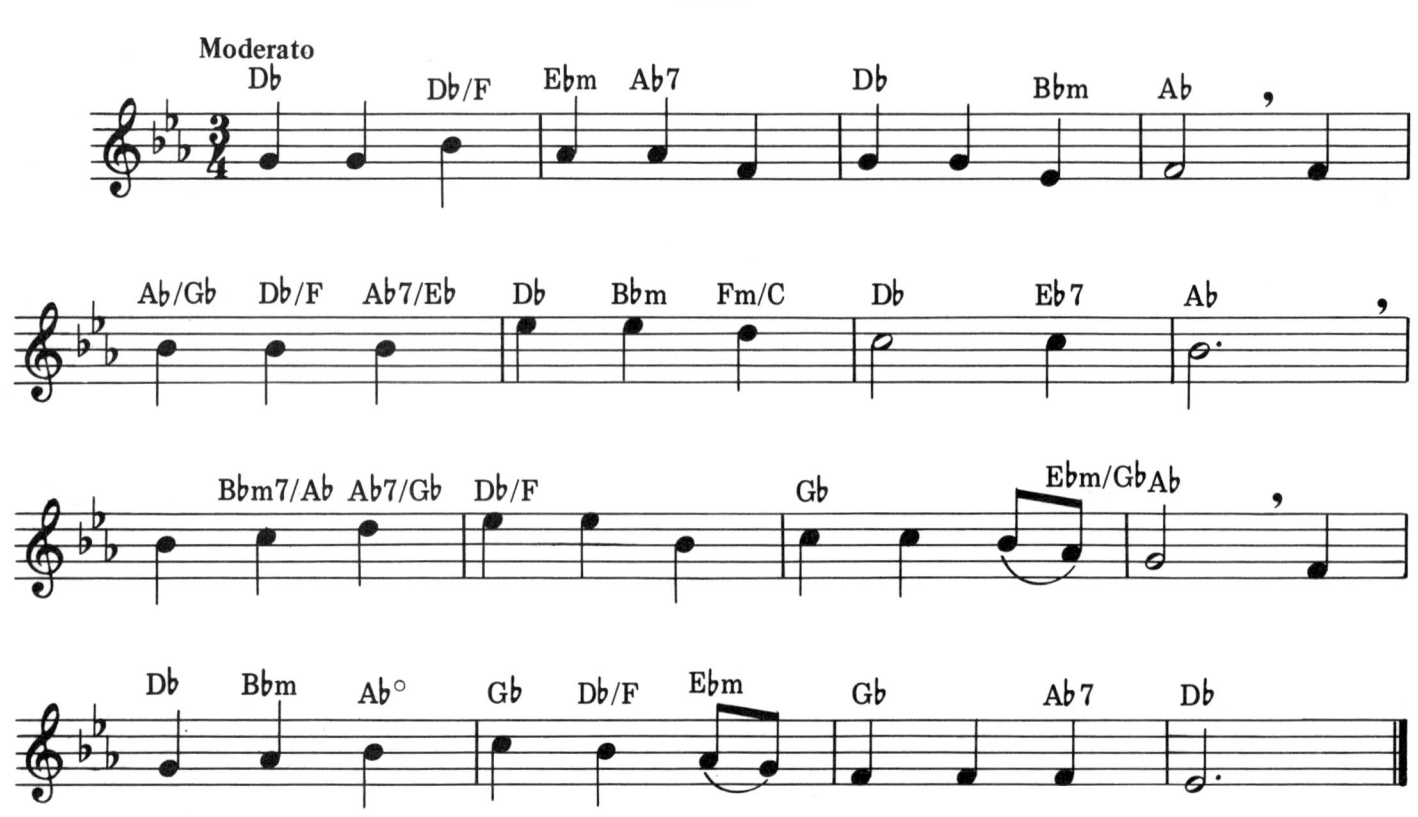

Masters In This Hall

Traditional French tune

Jingle Bells

James Pierpont

Noël De Cour
Traditional

O Sanctissima
from Tatersall's *Psalmody,* 1794

No Room In The Inn
Traditional

Little Jesus (Rocking)
Traditional

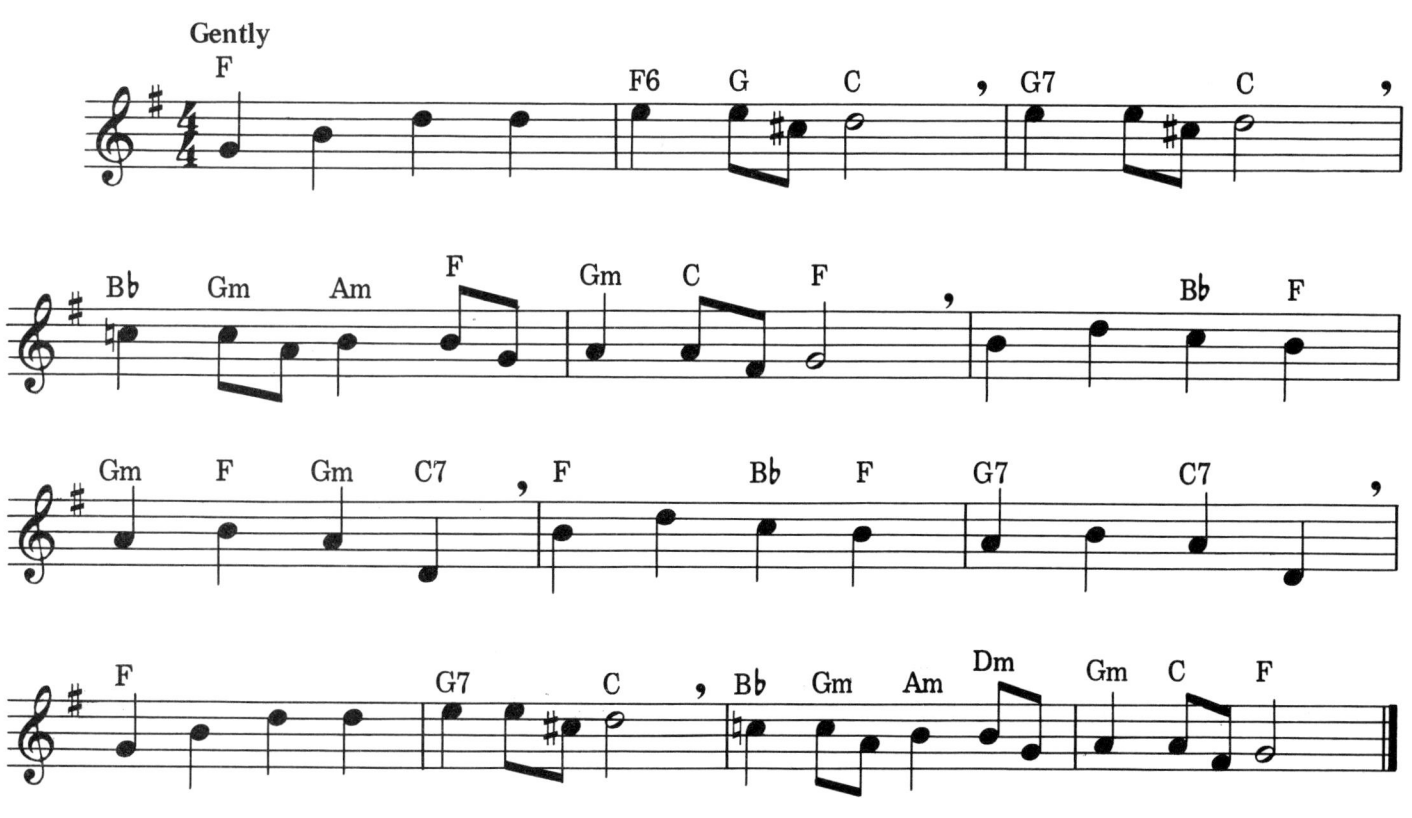

The Perfect Rose
Traditional

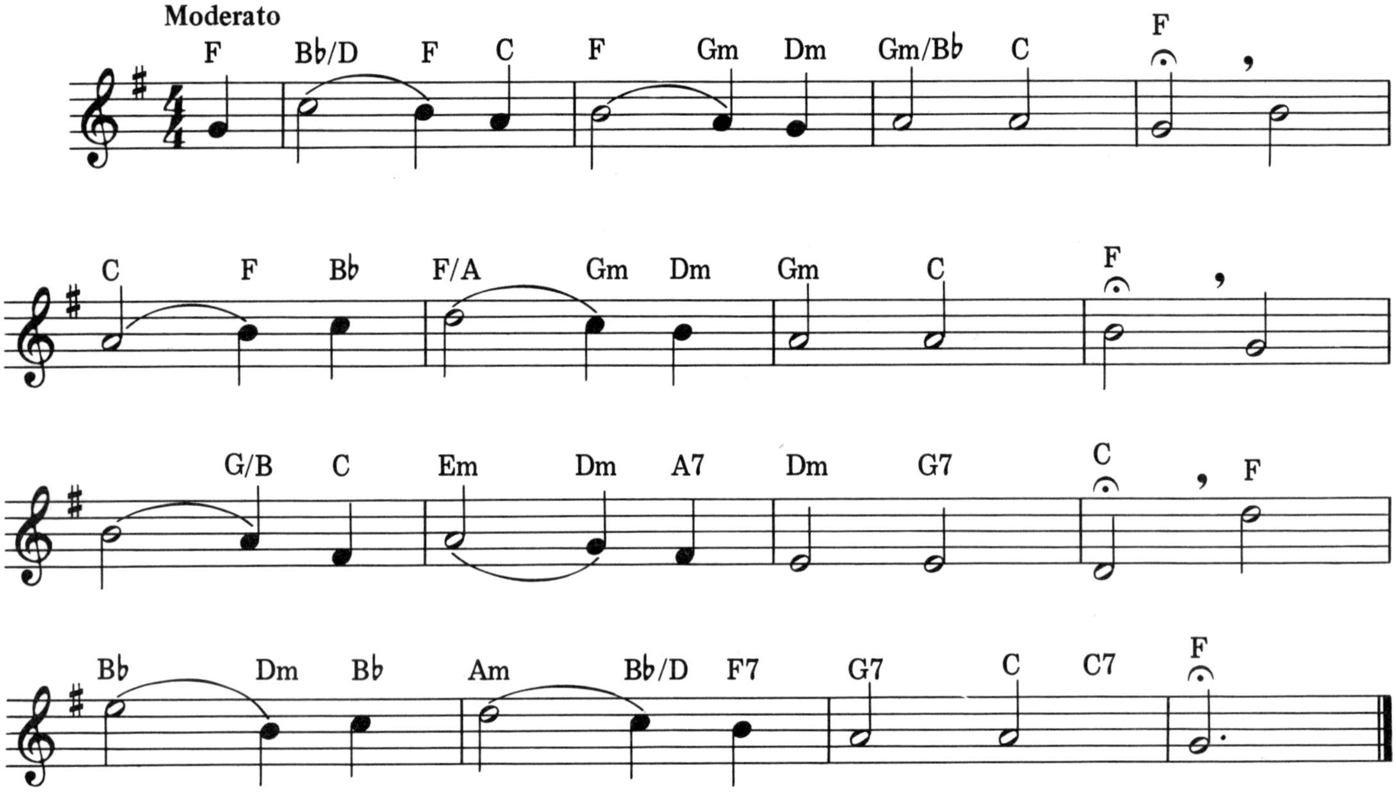

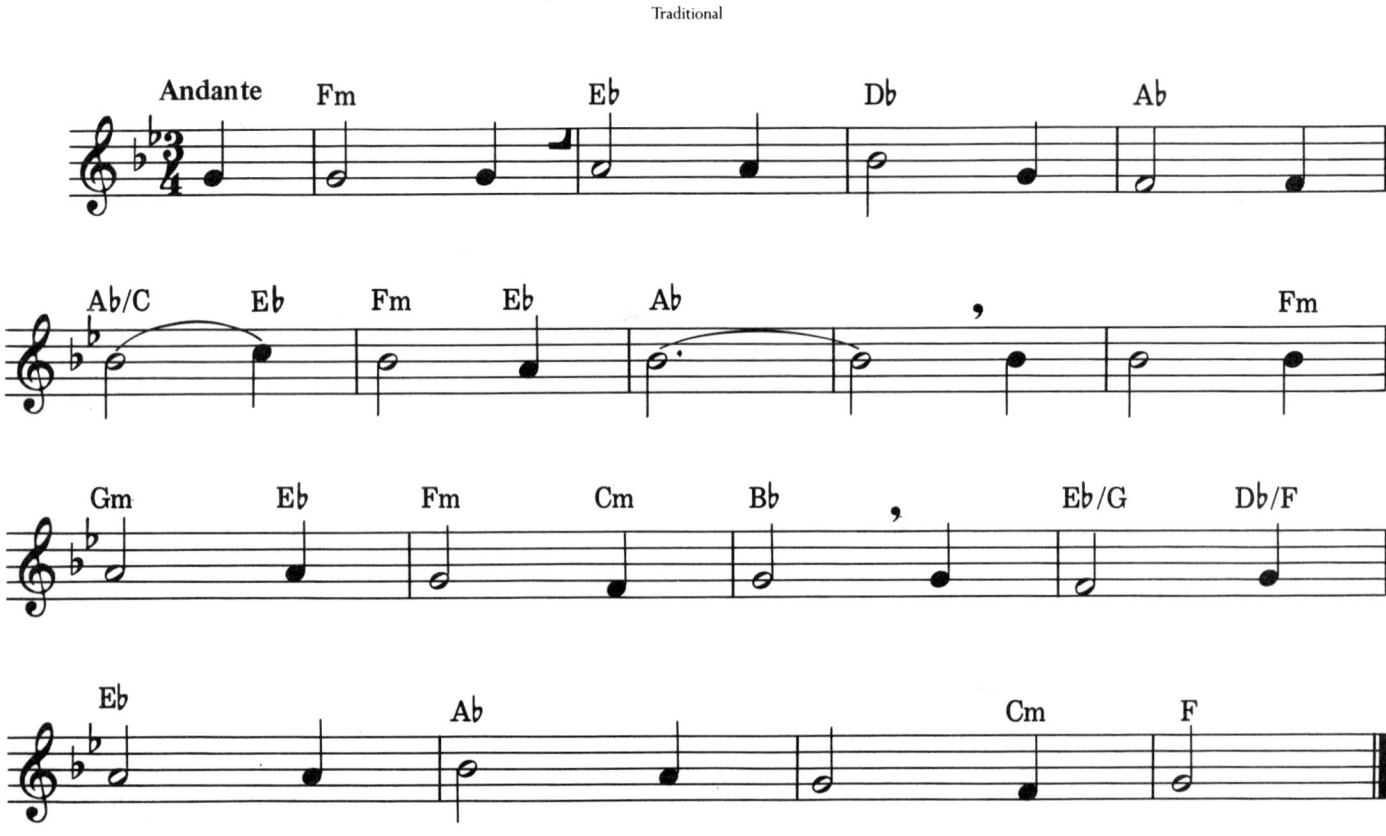

Puer Natus
Traditional

Silent Night
Franz Gruber, 1787–1863

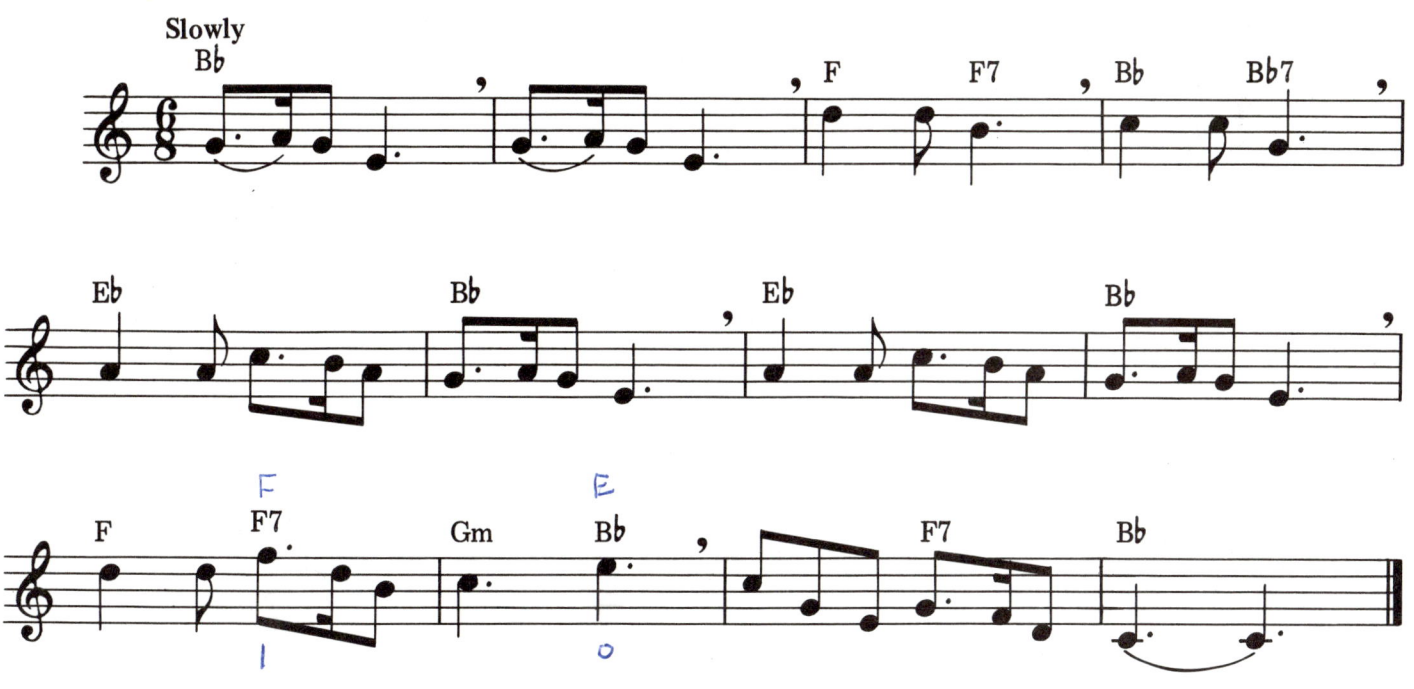

Past Three O'Clock
Traditional

O Christmas Tree
Traditional German carol

Quem Pastores
Traditional

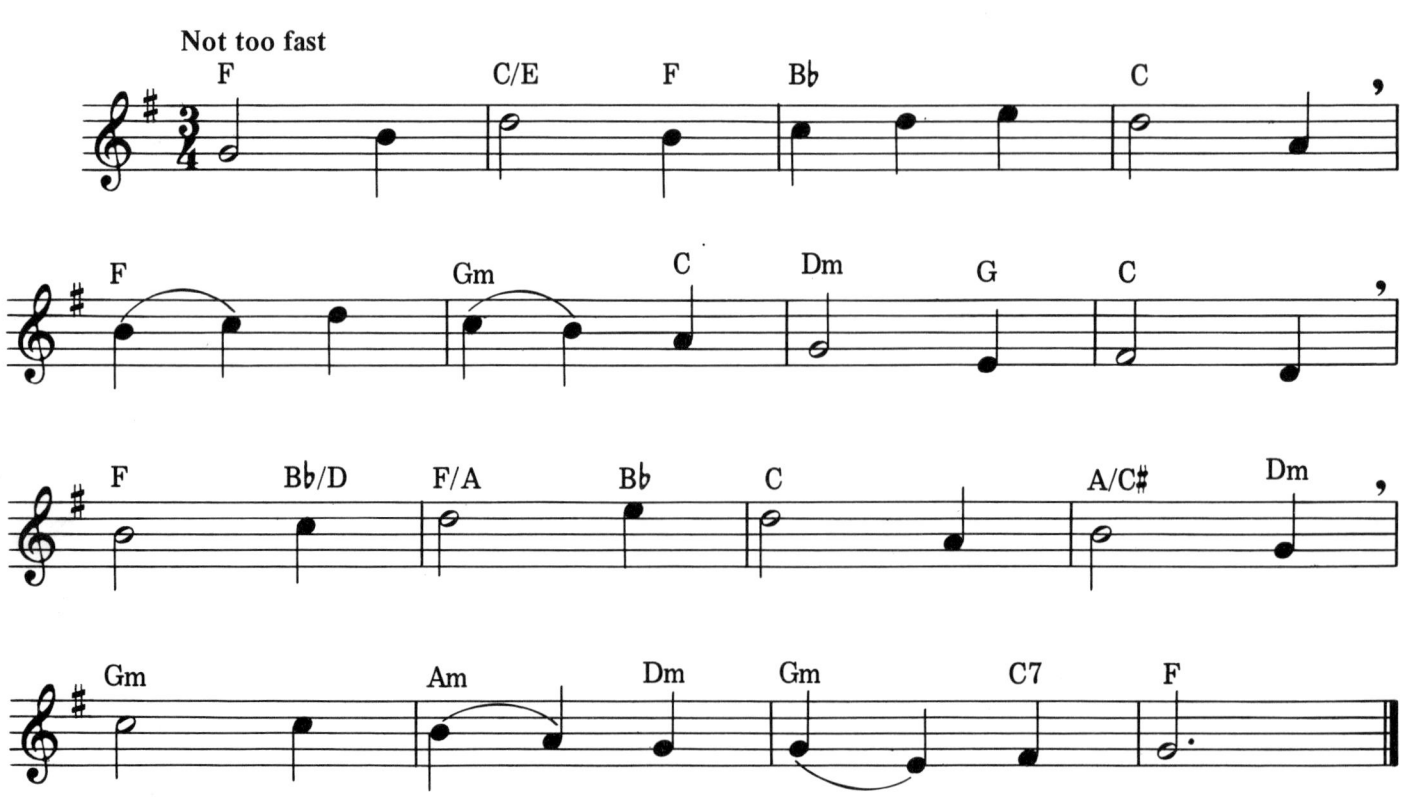

Righteous Joseph
Traditional

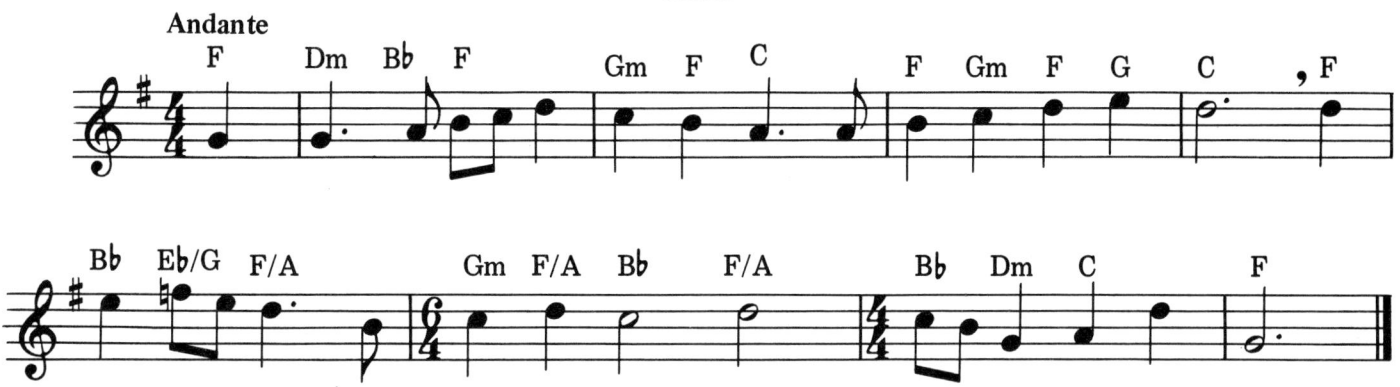

What Child Is This? (Greensleeves)
Traditional English tune

Refrain

Rise Up, Shepherd, And Follow

Negro spiritual

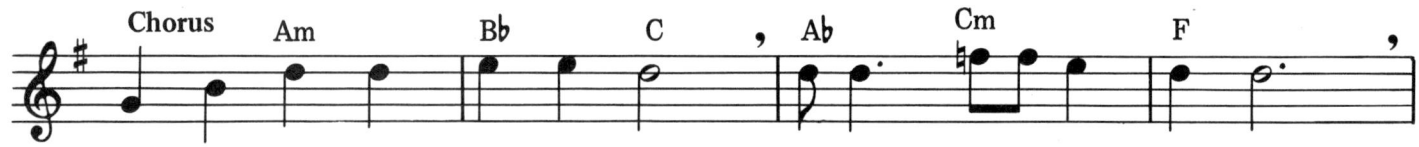

See Amid The Winter's Snow
Traditional

This Endris Night
Traditional

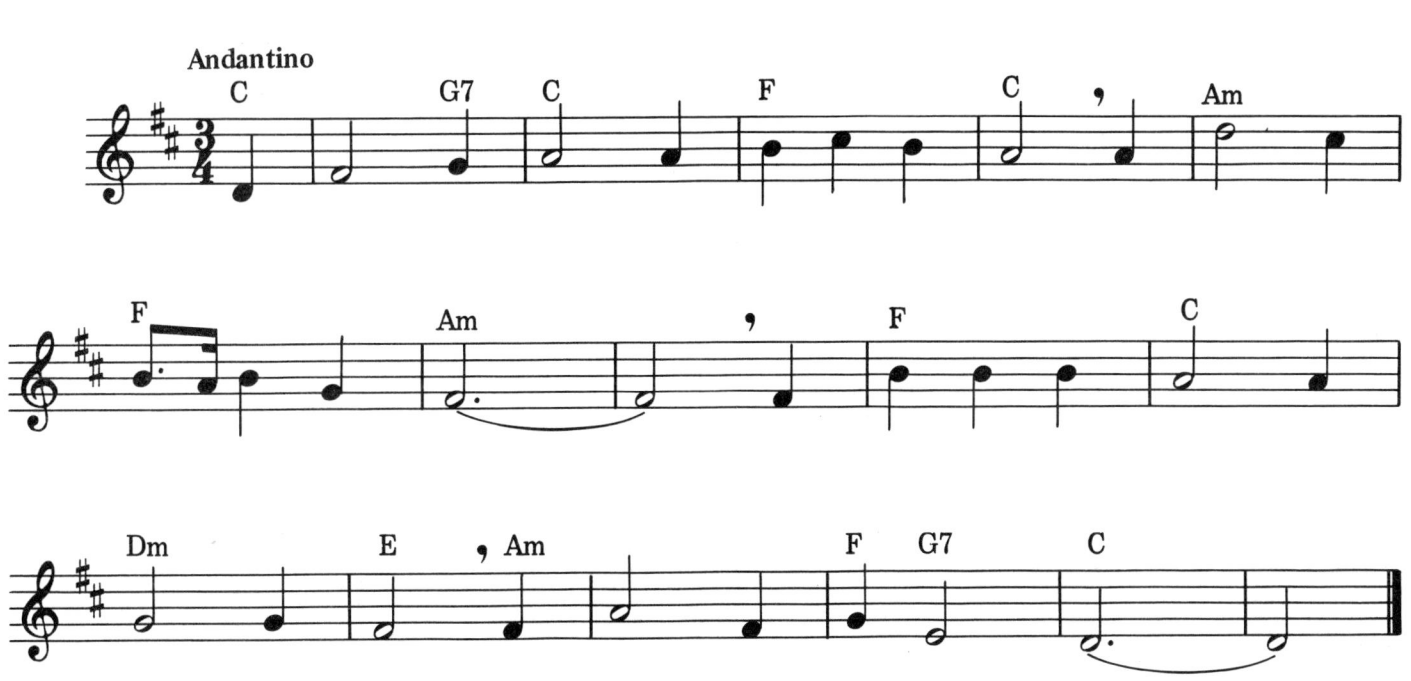

Star Of The East
A. Kennedy

Sleep, My Child Jesus
Traditional

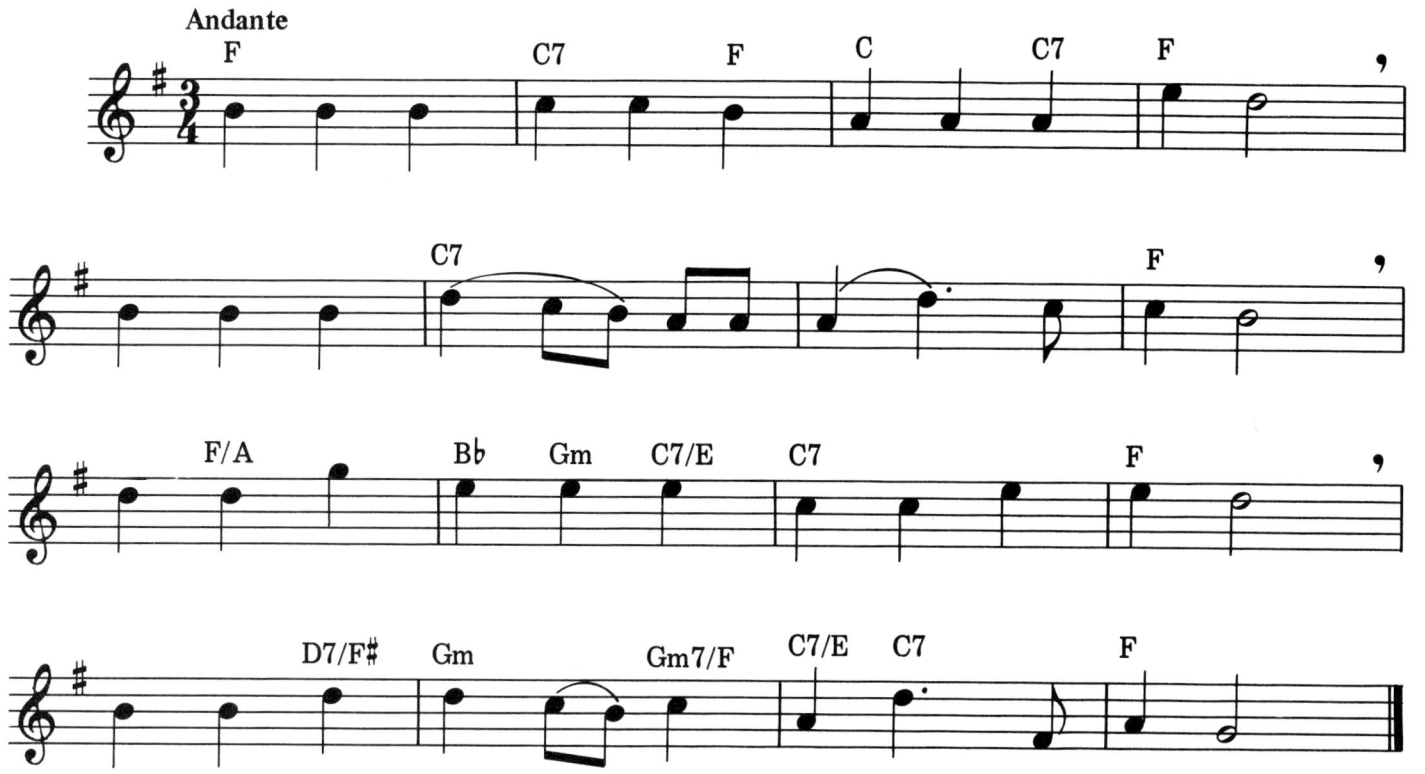

Up On The Housetop
B.R. Hanby

Wassail Song
Traditional English carol

Wexford Carol
Traditional English carol

O Little Town Of Bethlehem (Version 1)
Lewis H. Redner, 1831–1908

O Little Town Of Bethlehem (Version 2)
Traditional

We Three Kings
John H. Hopkins, Jr., 1820–1891

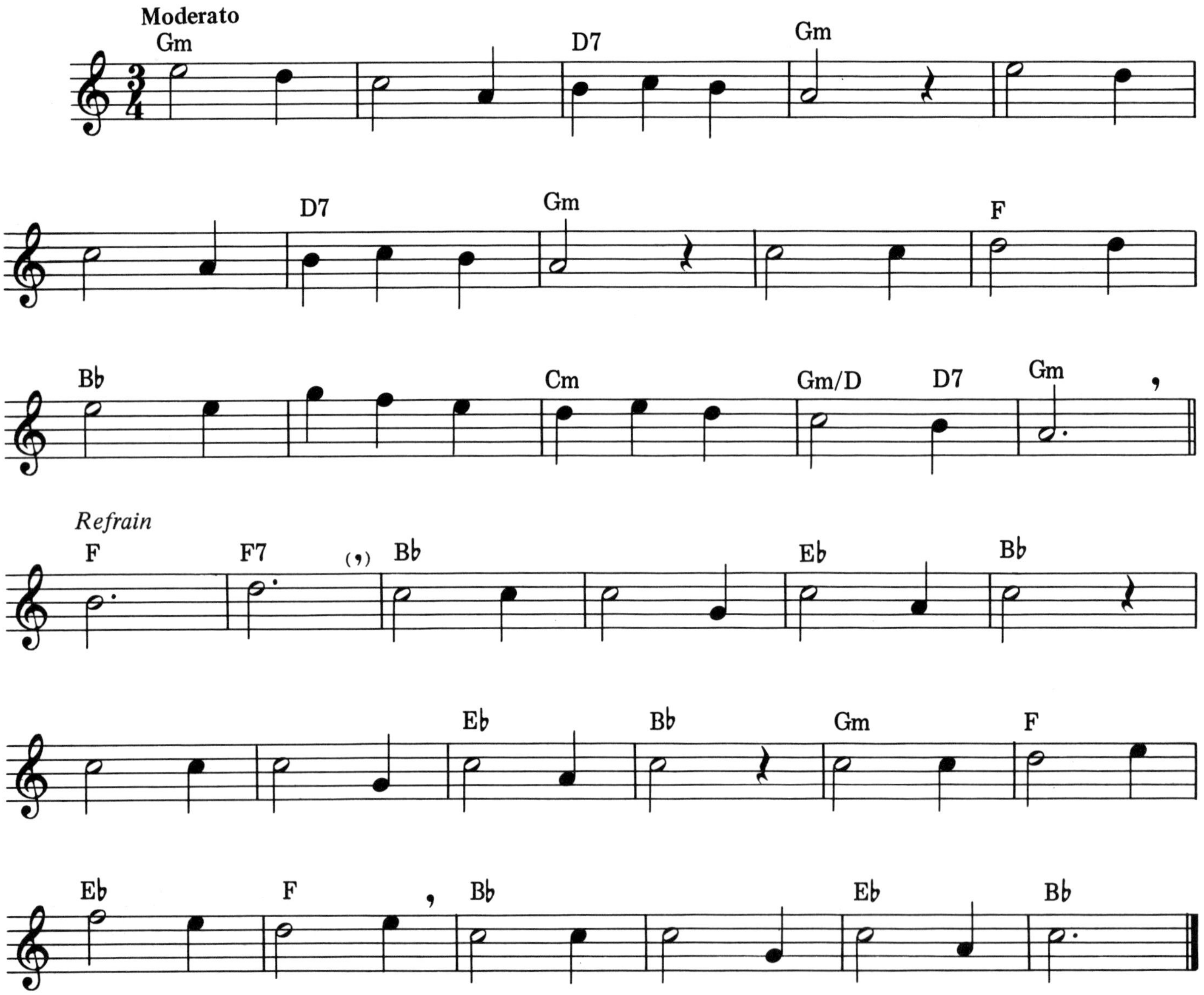

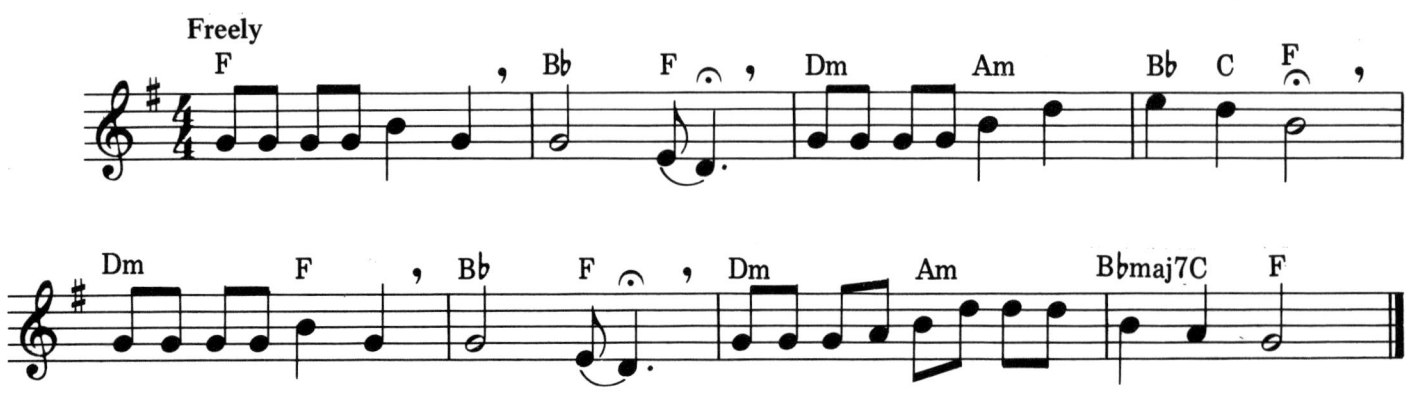

Mary Had A Baby
Negro spiritual

Song Of The Ship
Traditional

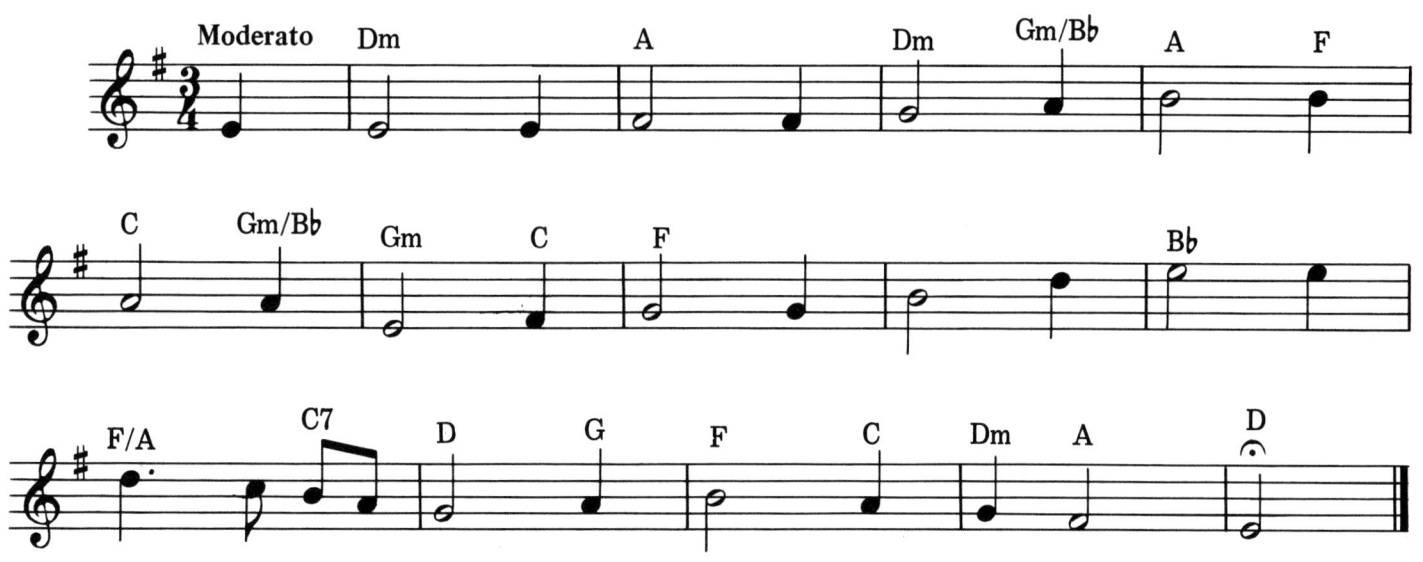

O Come, O Come, Emmanuel
adapted from plainsong by Thomas Helmore, 1811–1890

The Seven Joys Of Mary
Traditional

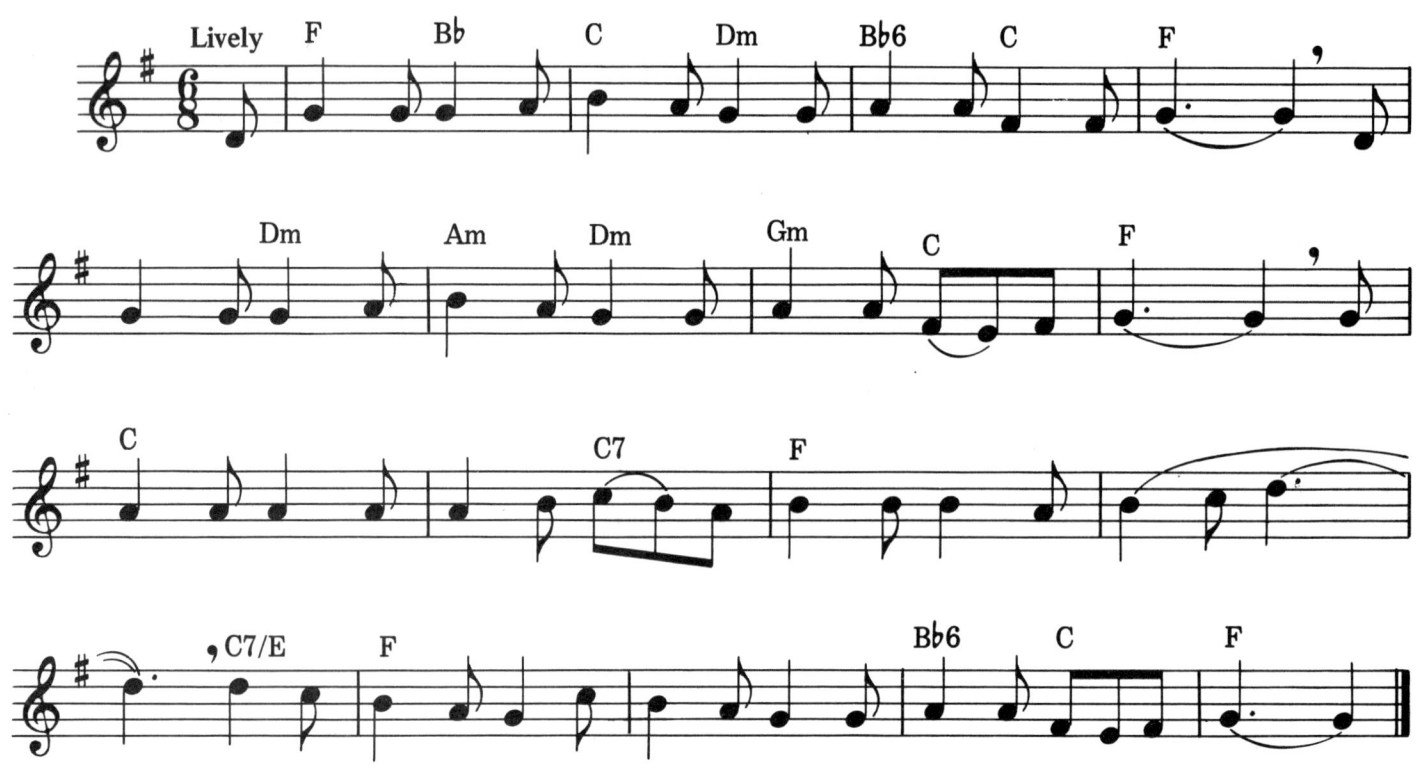

When Christ Was Born Of Mary Free
Arthur H. Brown

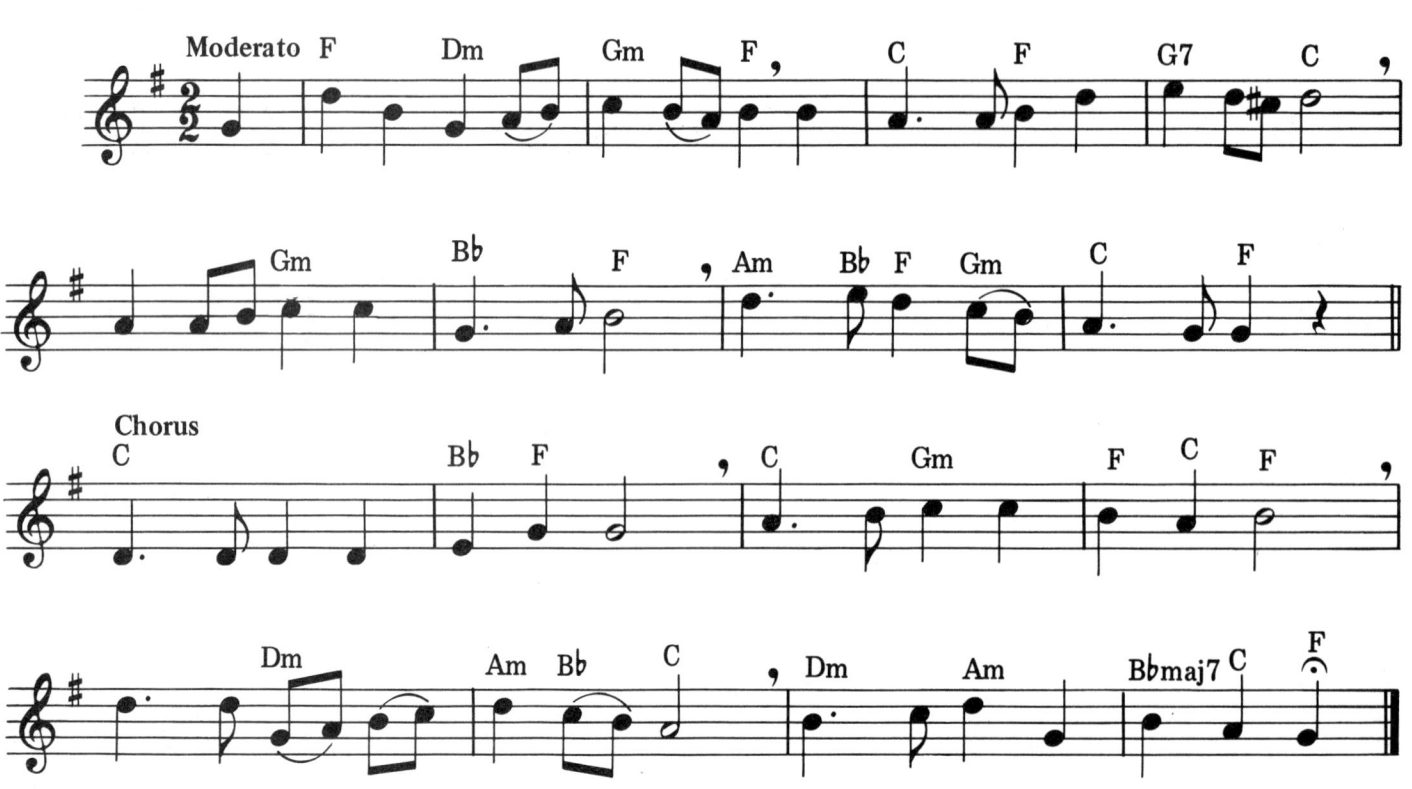

The World's Desire
Traditional

We Wish You A Merry Christmas
Traditional English carol